Please visit our website, www.garethstevens.com. For a free color catalog of all our high-quality books, call toll free 1-800-542-2595 or fax 1-877-542-2596.

Library of Congress Cataloging-in-Publication Data

Names: Rajczak, Michael, author.
Title: What are checks and balances? / Michael Rajczak.
Description: New York : Gareth Stevens Publishing, 2022. | Series: U.S. government Q & A! | Includes index.
Identifiers: LCCN 2020033533 (print) | LCCN 2020033534 (ebook) | ISBN 9781538264232 (library binding) | ISBN 9781538264218 (paperback) | ISBN 9781538264225 (set) | ISBN 9781538264249 (ebook)
Subjects: LCSH: Separation of powers–United States–Juvenile literature.
Classification: LCC JK305 .R35 2022 (print) | LCC JK305 (ebook) | DDC 320.473/04–dc23
LC record available at https://lccn.loc.gov/2020033533
LC ebook record available at https://lccn.loc.gov/2020033534

First Edition

Published in 2022 by
Gareth Stevens Publishing
29 E. 21st Street
New York, NY 10010

Copyright © 2022 Gareth Stevens Publishing

Designer: Andrea Davison-Bartolotta
Editor: Charlie Light

Photo credits: Cover (main) J Main/Shutterstock.com; cover (top inset) Steven Frame/Shutterstock.com; cover (bottom inset) Sagittarius Pro/Shutterstock.com; series art (paper, feather) Incomible/Shutterstock.com; series art (blue banner, red banner, stars) pingbat/Shutterstock.com; p. 5 Wikimedia Commons/File:Ruth Bader Ginsburg 2016 portrait.jpg; p. 6 Joe Ravi/Shutterstock.com; p. 7 mark reinstein/Shutterstock.com; pp. 9 (pins), 19 (pins) Alexander Limbach/Shutterstock.com; p. 9 (main) courtesy of Library of Congress; p. 10 Shawn Thew-Pool/Getty Images; p. 11 Jim Watson/AFP via Getty Images; p. 13 Lance7/Shutterstock.com; p. 15 Win McNamee/Getty Images; p. 17 Drew Angerer/Getty Images; p. 18 Wikimedia Commons/File:NRA member, we do our part.jpg; p. 19 (main) Wikimedia Commons/ File:NRA-Blue Eagle Emblem-poster displayed in restaurant window stating their participation and support for government... – NARA - 196519.tif; p. 21 JPL Designs/Shutterstock.com;

All rights reserved. No part of this book may be reproduced in any form without permission in writing from the publisher, except by a reviewer.

Printed in the United States of America

Some of the images in this book illustrate individuals who are models. The depictions do not imply actual situations or events.

CPSIA compliance information: Batch #CSGS22: For further information contact Gareth Stevens, New York, New York at 1-800-542-2595.

Contents

Why We Have Checks and Balances.............4
The Three Branches.............6
Powers of the Executive Branch.............8
More Powers to the President.............10
Checks on the Executive Branch.............12
Judicial Checks Executive.............14
Legislative Checks Judicial.............16
Judicial Checks Legislative.............18
The State of Checks and Balances.............20
Glossary.............22
For More Information.............23
Index.............24

Words in the glossary appear in **bold** type the first time they are used in the text.

Why We Have Checks and Balances

In May 1787, Americans had won their independence. Now it was time to set up a new government. The writers of the U.S. **Constitution** knew they didn't want to put too much power into the hands of one leader. Instead they created a government with three parts: the executive, legislative, and judicial branches.

The branches were meant to hold equal power. Each branch of government has some power over the other two. Today, these are called checks and balances.

Government Guides

"A constitution, as important as it is, will mean nothing unless the people are yearning for [wanting] liberty and freedom."
–Associate Justice of the Supreme Court, Ruth Bader Ginsburg

Associate Justice Ruth Bader Ginsburg served on the Supreme Court from 1993 until her death in 2020. The Supreme Court is the highest court of the judicial branch.

The Three Branches

The executive branch of government includes the president. It also includes 15 different parts of the government, such as the Department of Education and the Department of State. The goal of the executive branch is to enforce, or make sure people obey, the law.

The legislative branch is Congress. Congress is made up of the House of Representatives and the Senate. Its main job is creating laws.

The judicial branch is made up of the Supreme Court and the **federal** courts. The Supreme Court has nine judges, known as justices.

Supreme Court

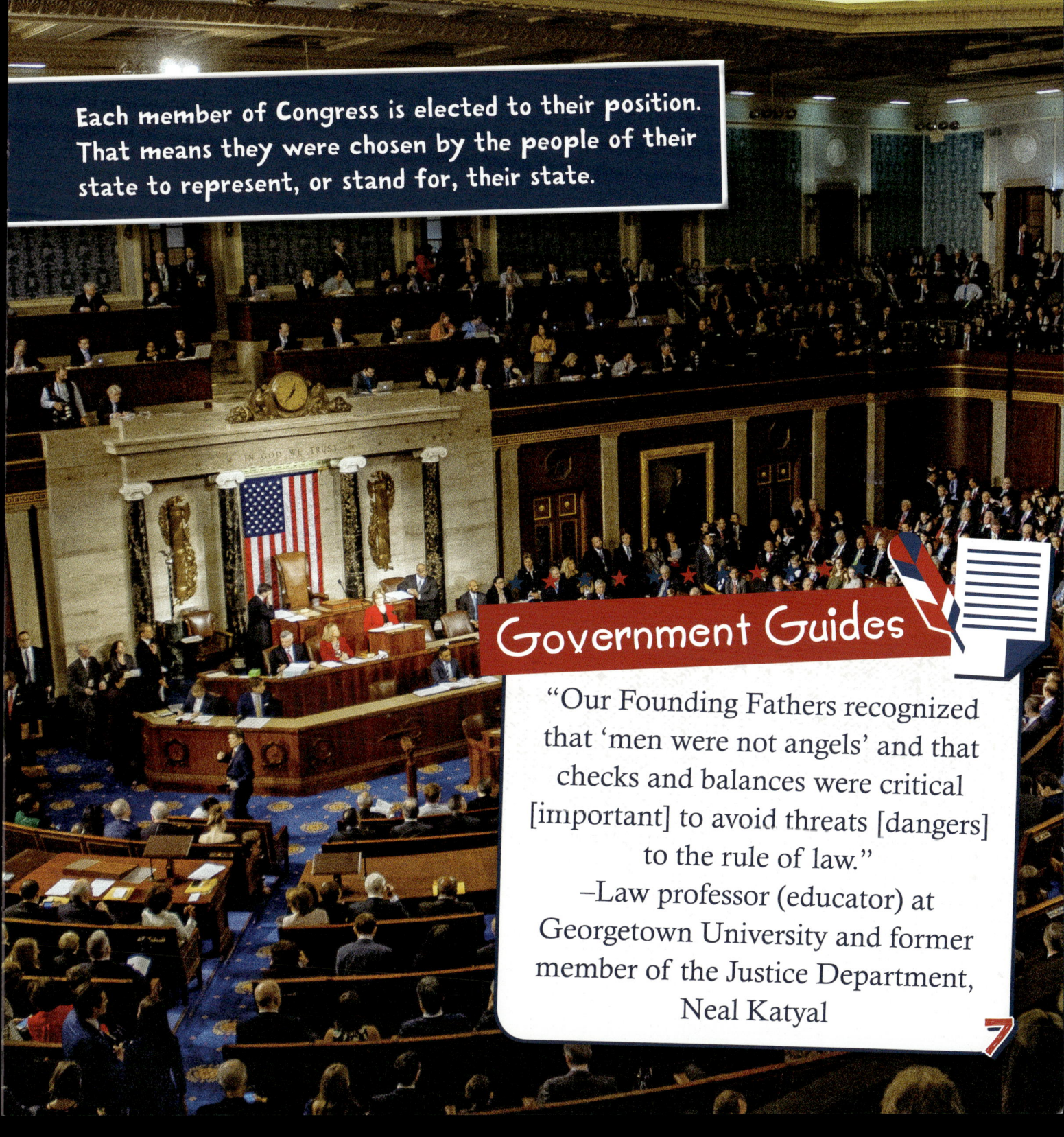

Each member of Congress is elected to their position. That means they were chosen by the people of their state to represent, or stand for, their state.

Government Guides

"Our Founding Fathers recognized that 'men were not angels' and that checks and balances were critical [important] to avoid threats [dangers] to the rule of law."
–Law professor (educator) at Georgetown University and former member of the Justice Department, Neal Katyal

Powers of the Executive Branch

The president's powers come from the Constitution. It says the president can sign a bill into law after it is passed by Congress. Presidents can also check Congress's ability to pass a law by **vetoing** a bill. A pocket veto also ends a bill if the president doesn't sign it for 10 days and Congress stops meeting within that time.

The vice president can also check Congress's power. If a vote for a bill is a tie in the Senate, the vice president's vote can break it.

Government Guides

Government expert, or authority, Todd Gaziano said this about the way a president may carry out laws: "He has not only the power, but also the responsibility to see that the Constitution and laws are **interpreted** correctly."

The president can call Congress into session, or meeting, for a special reason. In 1948, President Harry Truman called back Congress for the "Turnip Day" session, on a day when turnips are harvested, to pass important laws.

More Powers to the President

The executive branch has powers that greatly affect and check the judicial branch too. The president nominates, or chooses, the people who could serve as federal judges. This includes Supreme Court justices. A president will often pick people who think about government the way they do.

Another check on the judicial branch is the president's power to pardon, or excuse, people found guilty of crimes. That means a person sentenced by the courts for breaking the law does not have to complete their sentence, or punishment.

President Obama signs a bill into a law.

President Donald Trump nominated Brett Kavanaugh to be a Supreme Court justice.

11

Checks on the Executive Branch

One way the legislative branch checks the power of the president is by passing laws that limit what presidents can do. In 1951, Congress passed an **amendment** stating presidents may only serve up to two four-year terms. Also, if two-thirds of each house in Congress votes to override a president's veto, the bill becomes law. Congress controls the executive branch's federal money too with "the power of the purse."

Though a president can create **treaties**, the Senate must approve them. The Senate must also approve the president's **appointments** for federal judges and Supreme Court justices.

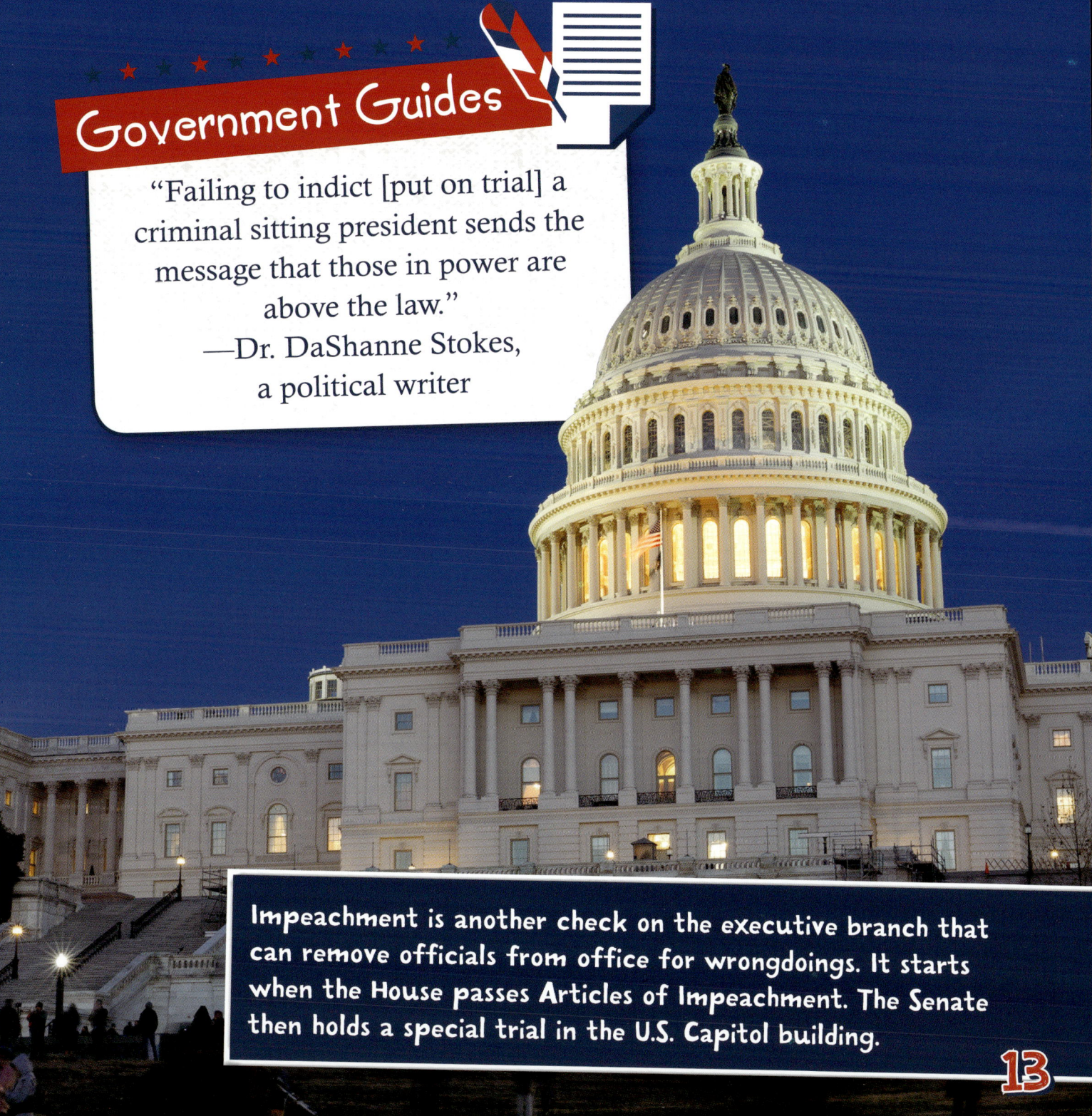

Government Guides

"Failing to indict [put on trial] a criminal sitting president sends the message that those in power are above the law."
—Dr. DaShanne Stokes, a political writer

Impeachment is another check on the executive branch that can remove officials from office for wrongdoings. It starts when the House passes Articles of Impeachment. The Senate then holds a special trial in the U.S. Capitol building.

Judicial Checks Executive

The judicial branch, often the Supreme Court, has the power to rule actions of the executive branch unconstitutional. This is called judicial review and it started with the 1803 case of *Marbury v. Madison*. Judicial review means that the judicial branch can decide if a law or president's action goes against the Constitution.

This happened in 1952 when President Harry Truman wanted the government to take over the nation's steel mills during the **Korean War**. The Supreme Court said the Constitution doesn't give presidents this power.

When the Supreme Court issues a ruling, it is often very big news. These reporters are shown running with news of a new Supreme Court ruling in 2013.

Legislative Checks Judicial

The Senate's ability to approve a new judge is also a check on the judicial branch. The Senate makes such a decision after investigating, or looking into, who the person is. Does this person have the education and experience to be a good judge? If the Senate votes in favor of that person, then they are allowed to take the job.

Congress also has the power to remove poor judges. In 2010, G. Thomas Porteous Jr. was removed because he accepted **bribes**.

Government Guides

Founding Father James Madison wrote in favor of the Constitution's checks and balances. He wrote specifically ". . . you must first enable the government to control the governed; and in the next place oblige [allow] it to control itself."

Before becoming a Supreme Court justice, Neil Gorsuch answered questions from members of the Senate.

Judicial Checks Legislative

The judicial branch checks the power of the legislative branch. It does this by ruling laws unconstitutional.

During the **Great Depression**, Congress passed many laws to help the nation recover. The Supreme Court ruled two of these unconstitutional. One was the National Industrial Recovery Act (NIRA) because it gave some of Congress's power to a group called the National Recovery Administration (NRA). The judges also stopped the Agricultural Adjustment Act that helped farmers because they thought agriculture, or farming, was not part of the federal government's responsibility.

National Recovery Administration poster

Government Guides

"We are under a Constitution, but the Constitution is what the judges say it is."
—Charles Evans Hughes, Chief Justice of the Supreme Court during the time of the Great Depression.

The National Recovery Administration, part of the NIRA, was a government office that worked with companies to make rules for business practices. It was ruled unconstitutional by the Supreme Court.

The State of Checks and Balances

The writers of the Constitution wanted to make sure no branch of government could abuse, or harmfully misuse, its power. However, some have argued that checks and balances make government decisions too slow. They can cause a stalemate, or situation in which no progress can be made.

Some people also argue that the system of checks and balances no longer works. The branches, often the executive branch, have found ways around the checks. Still, checks and balances are a big part of how the U.S. government runs today!

Think About It!

How have the need for checks and balances changed from the founding of the United States to today?

Powers of the Three Branches

 Legislative branch	 Executive branch	 Judicial branch
Pass laws	Veto laws	Declare laws unconstitutional
Declare (state officially or publicly) war	Order armed forces	Hear cases on federal law
Impeach president and federal officials	Grant pardons	Rule over impeachment trials
Approve presidential appointments	Appoint judges, **ambassadors**, department heads	Declare presidential acts unconstitutional
Sign treaties	Handle matters with other countries, make treaties	
Make taxes		
Set number of Supreme Court justices		
Control Supreme Court's **jurisdiction**		

> The system of checks and balances isn't perfect. Do you think it has stopped any one branch from becoming too powerful?

Glossary

ambassador: a high-ranking person who represents their government in another country

amendment: a change or addition to a constitution

appointment: the act of giving a certain job to someone. To appoint is to choose someone for a certain job or duty.

bribe: something, such as money, given to a person to get them to do something

constitution: the basic laws by which a country or state is governed

federal: having to do with the national government

Great Depression: a period of economic troubles with widespread unemployment and poverty (1929–1939)

interpret: to explain something's meaning

jurisdiction: the authority or right to govern an area. Also, the power to make judgments about the law.

Korean War: a conflict between North and South Korea that began in 1950 and ended in 1953

treaty: an agreement between countries

veto: to officially reject or refuse a bill to become law. Also, the right of a person in charge to decide something will not be approved.

For More Information

Books

Kellaher, Karen. *The Presidency*. New York, NY: Children's Press, an imprint of Scholastic Inc., 2020.

Lawton, Cassie M. *Checks and Balances*. New York, NY: Cavendish Square Publishing, 2021.

Weber, Shannon. *Civics: Democracy Rules!*. New York, NY: Kingfisher, 2020.

Websites

BrainPOP Branches of Government
www.brainpop.com/socialstudies/usgovernment/branchesofgovernment/
Watch an animated video on how the U.S. government works at this cool site!

Impeachment: Britannica Kids
kids.britannica.com/kids/article/impeachment/390041
Take a closer look at how impeachment works at this site.

U.S. Government for Kids: Checks and Balances
www.ducksters.com/history/us_government/checks_and_balances.php
Check out more about checks and balances and take a quiz!

Publisher's note to educators and parents: Our editors have carefully reviewed these websites to ensure that they are suitable for students. Many websites change frequently, however, and we cannot guarantee that a site's future contents will continue to meet our high standards of quality and educational value. Be advised that students should be closely supervised whenever they access the internet.

Index

Agricultural Adjustment Act 18

bill 8, 12

Congress 6, 7, 8, 9, 12, 16, 18

Constitution 4, 8, 14, 16, 19, 20

executive branch 6, 10, 12, 13, 14, 20

farming 18

Gaziano, Todd 8

Ginsburg, Ruth Bader 4, 5

Gorsuch, Neil 17

Hughes, Charles Evans 19

impeachment 13

judge 6, 10, 12, 16, 18, 19

judicial branch 4, 5, 6, 10, 14, 16, 18

judicial review 14

Katyal, Neal 7

Kavanaugh, Brett 11

law 6, 7, 8, 9, 10, 12, 13, 14, 18

legislative branch 6, 12, 18

Madison, James 16

Marbury v. Madison 14

National Industrial Recovery Act (NIRA) 18, 19

pardon 10

Porteous, G. Thomas, Jr. 16

"power of the purse" 14

president 6, 8, 9, 10, 11, 12, 13, 14

reporters 15

Senate 6, 8, 12, 13, 16, 17

steel mills 14

Stokes, DaShanne 13

trial 13

Truman, Harry 9, 14

Trump, Donald 11

"Turnip Day" session 9

U.S. Capitol 13

vice president 8